This Create with Pinkee

Sweet Hallowe'en

Belongs To

....

Contents

Hello, my wonderful Pinkee Pals!

My intention with this book and series is to get you drawing, or creating something every day. There are so many benefits to having a creative hobby but sometimes the rest of our lives can push out those hobbies we enjoy.

With this book, the idea is to pick it up and do something. There is nothing in the book that will take you a long time, and nothing is meant to be finished pieces of art!
Have fun, don't take things too seriously and enjoy the experience of jumping in and creating with me.

Throughout the book, you will find many different things to help you create something! Whether that's a tutorial, a doodle prompt, or just colouring.

Enjoy and have fun creating with me!
With Love,
Pinkee

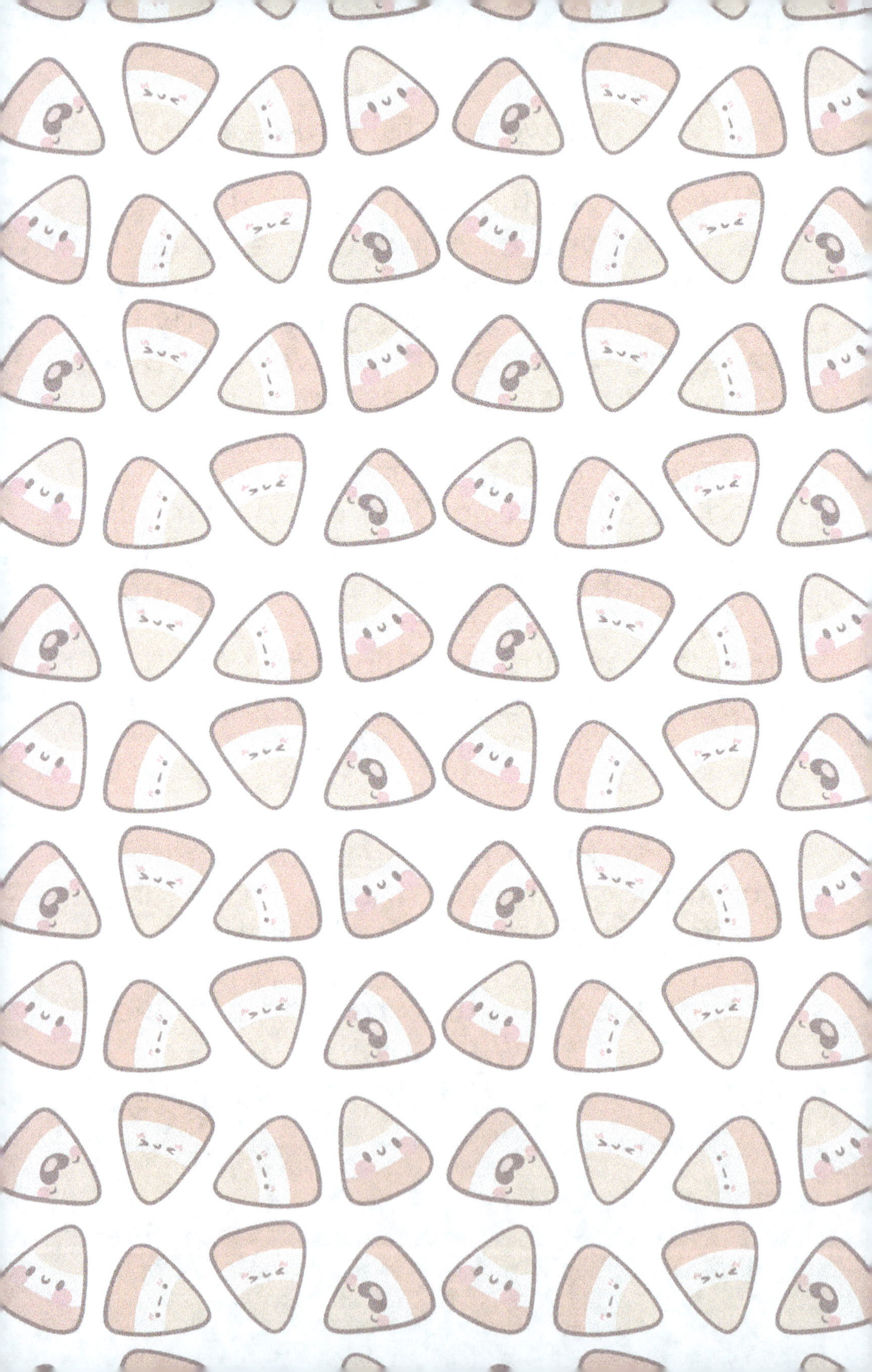

Faces
with Pinkee

Practice creating faces by carving adorable, sad, mean or mad expressions in the pumpkins below!

Colours
with Pinkee

Use these color palettes for this month to help you with your art practice.

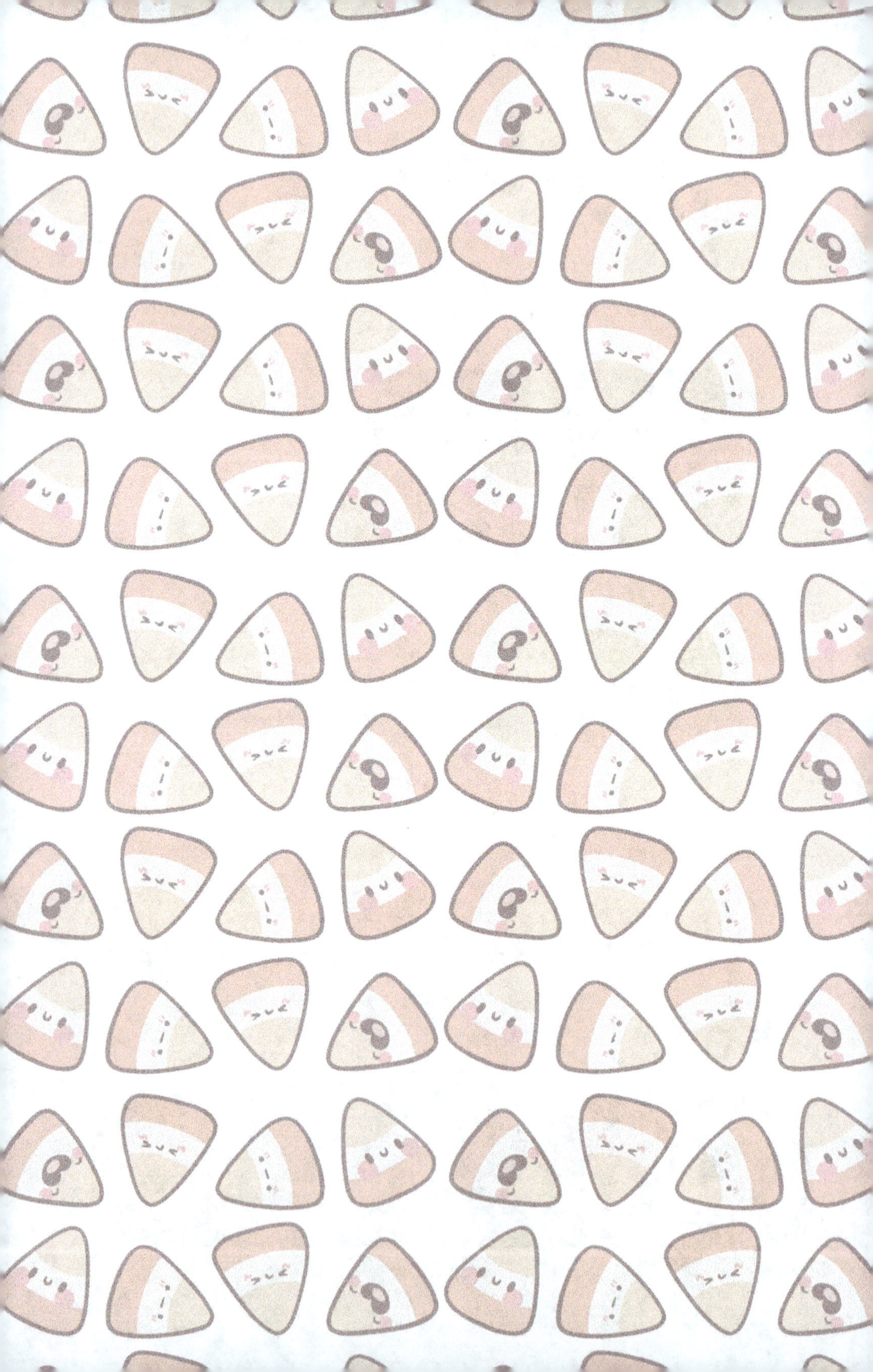

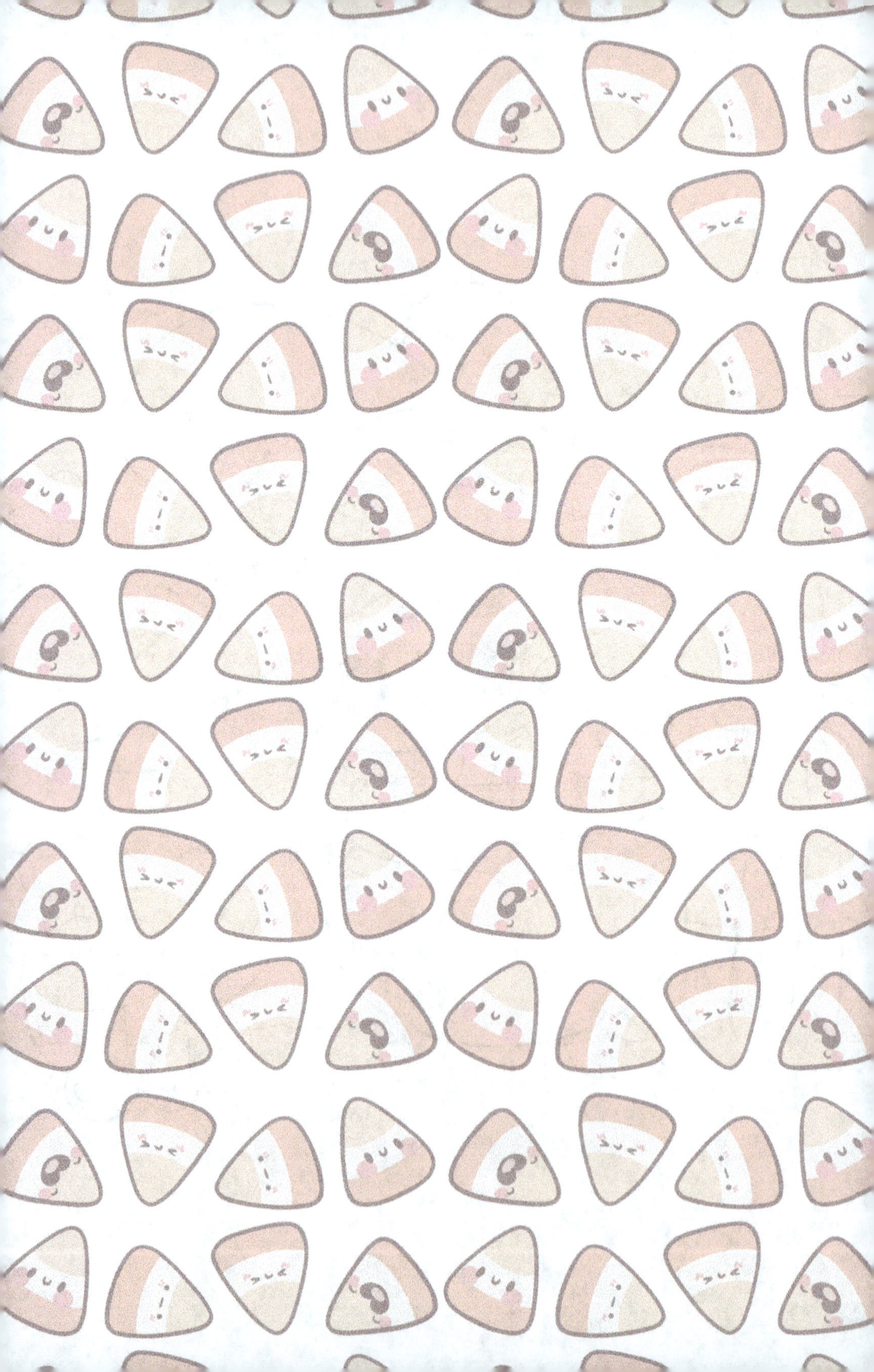

Learn
with Pinkee

Hello again my Pinkee Pal!

Over the next few pages you'll dive in with me as we learn some fun tricks, get in some tips and just practice our art.

Practice how to make patterns for your doodle art. (I tend to use these more for colouring than anything else!)

Each book in this series is a little different but at the end of this section you'll have new skills, and hopefullyill have had some fun as well!

Love,
Pinkee

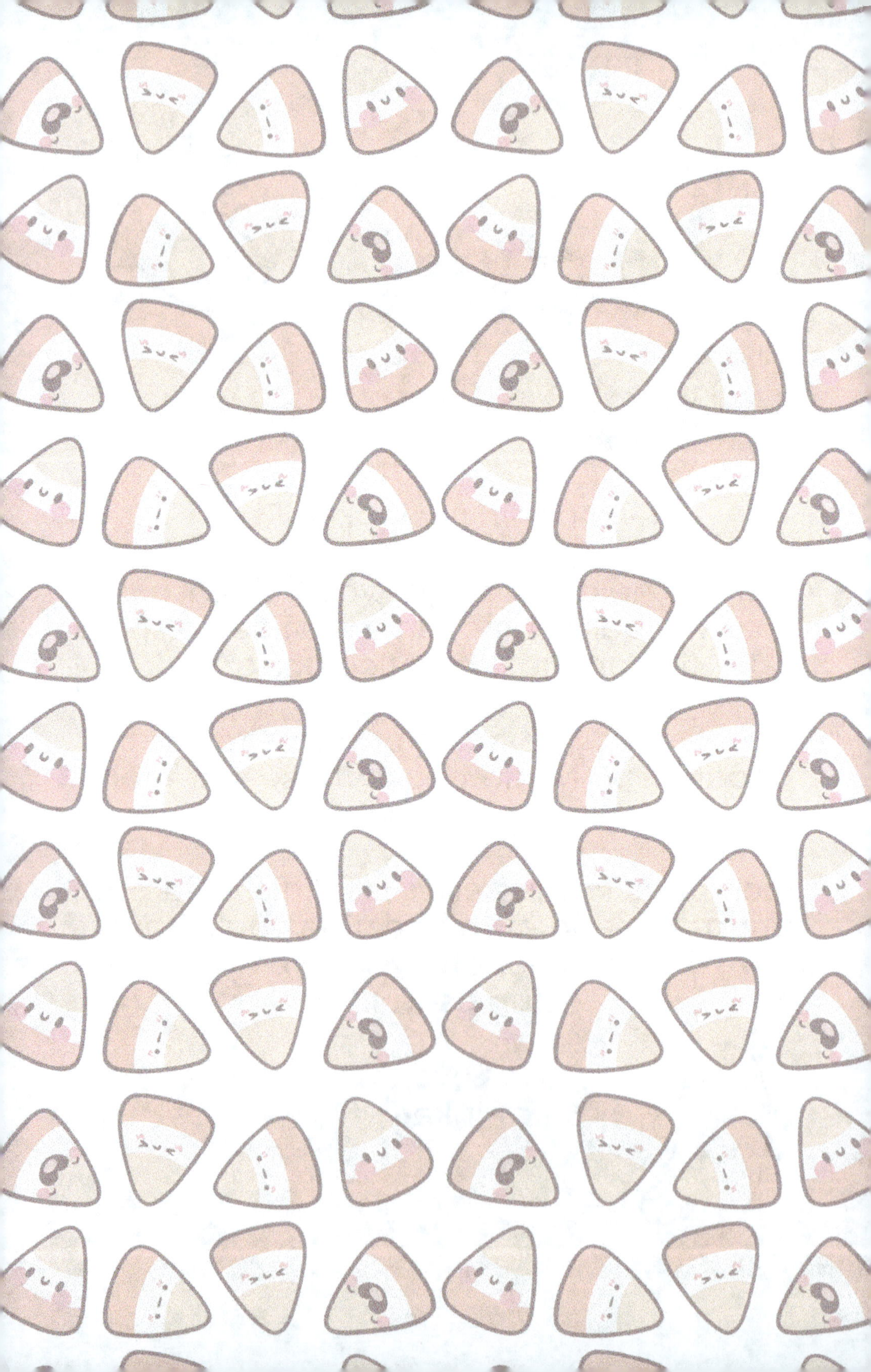

Patterns
with Pinkee

Practice drawing the following doodle patterns. These simple patterns can really ramp up your doodles!

Patterns

Now that you have the basics down, try creating
your own patterns in the blocks below!

Blobs
with Pinkee

Using the blobs below, have fun creating something with them!

Blobs
with Pinkee

Now that you have that down, create your own below!

Fun
with Pinkee

Time for some fun! Using a 6 sided die, create an adorable pumpkin patch with the options below.

Body Shape

Face

Stem

Accessory

Examples

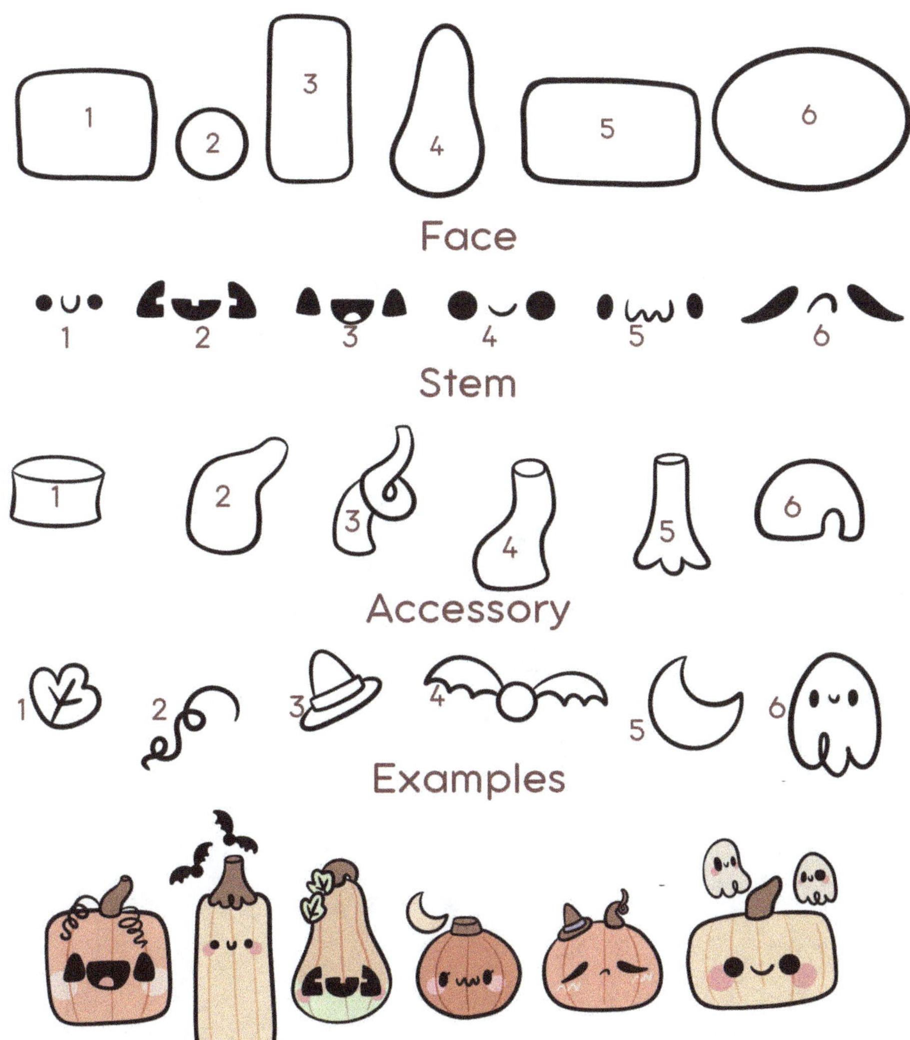

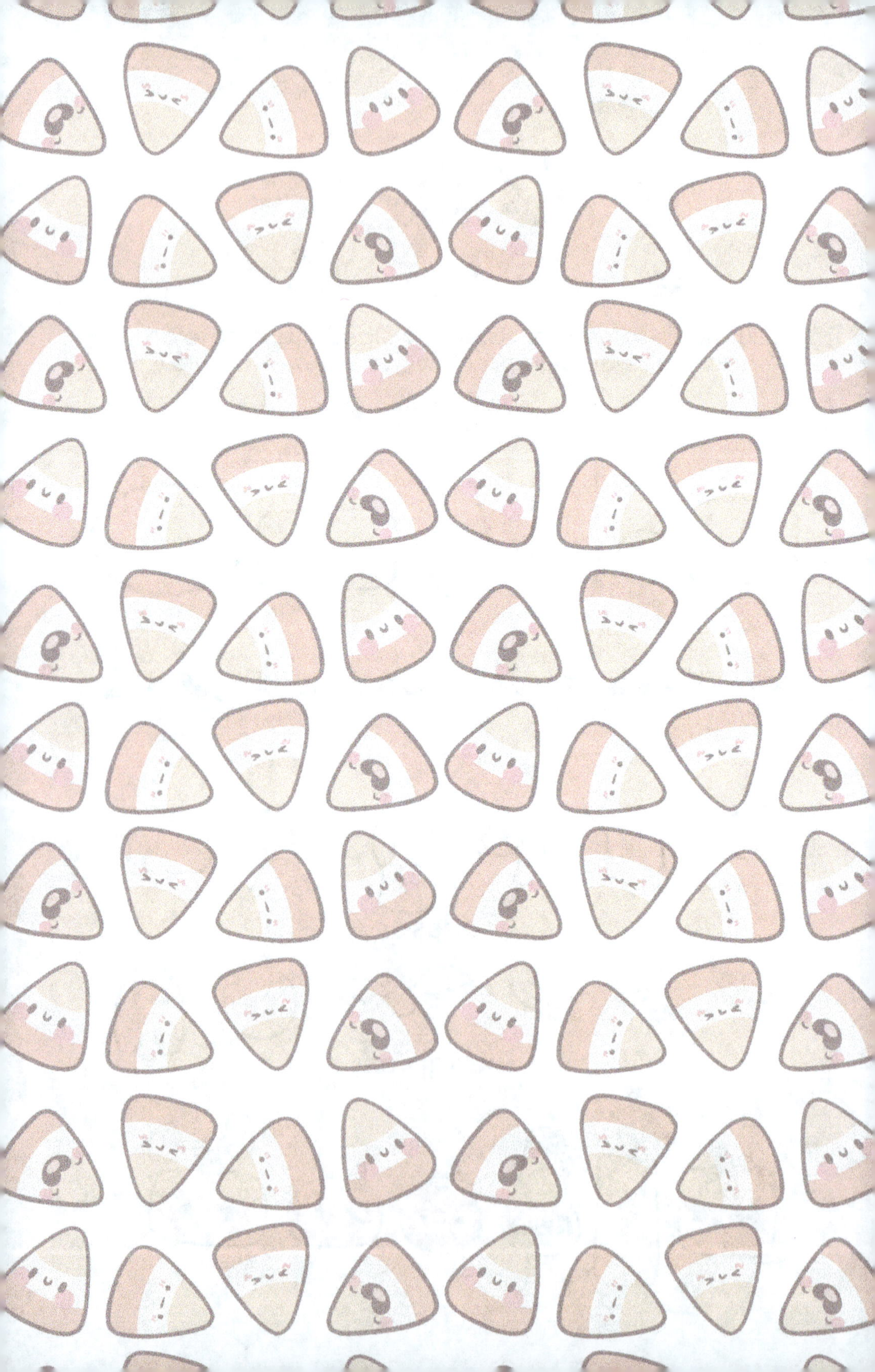

Use this page to create your pumpkin patch! Feel free to mix and match or add even more accessories!

Hello, my Pinkee Pals!

I think at this point if you know me, you know I love a mandala! I create a lot of them. A lot.

I started drawing them for my nephew during the pandemic and never stopped. It was the first book I ever created. So, of course, I needed to include them in this series.

I hope you enjoy these mandalas.

Hugs
Pinkee

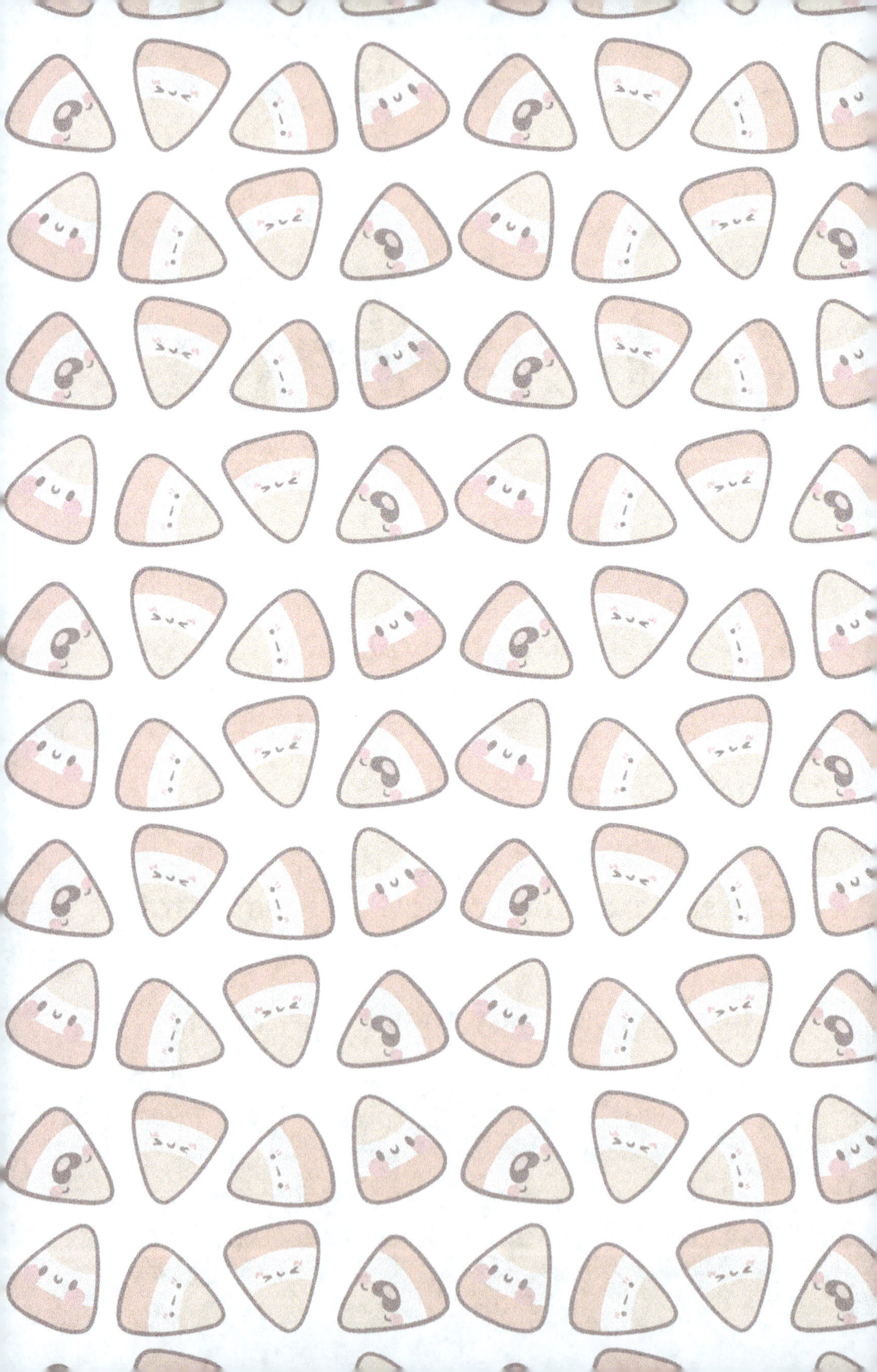

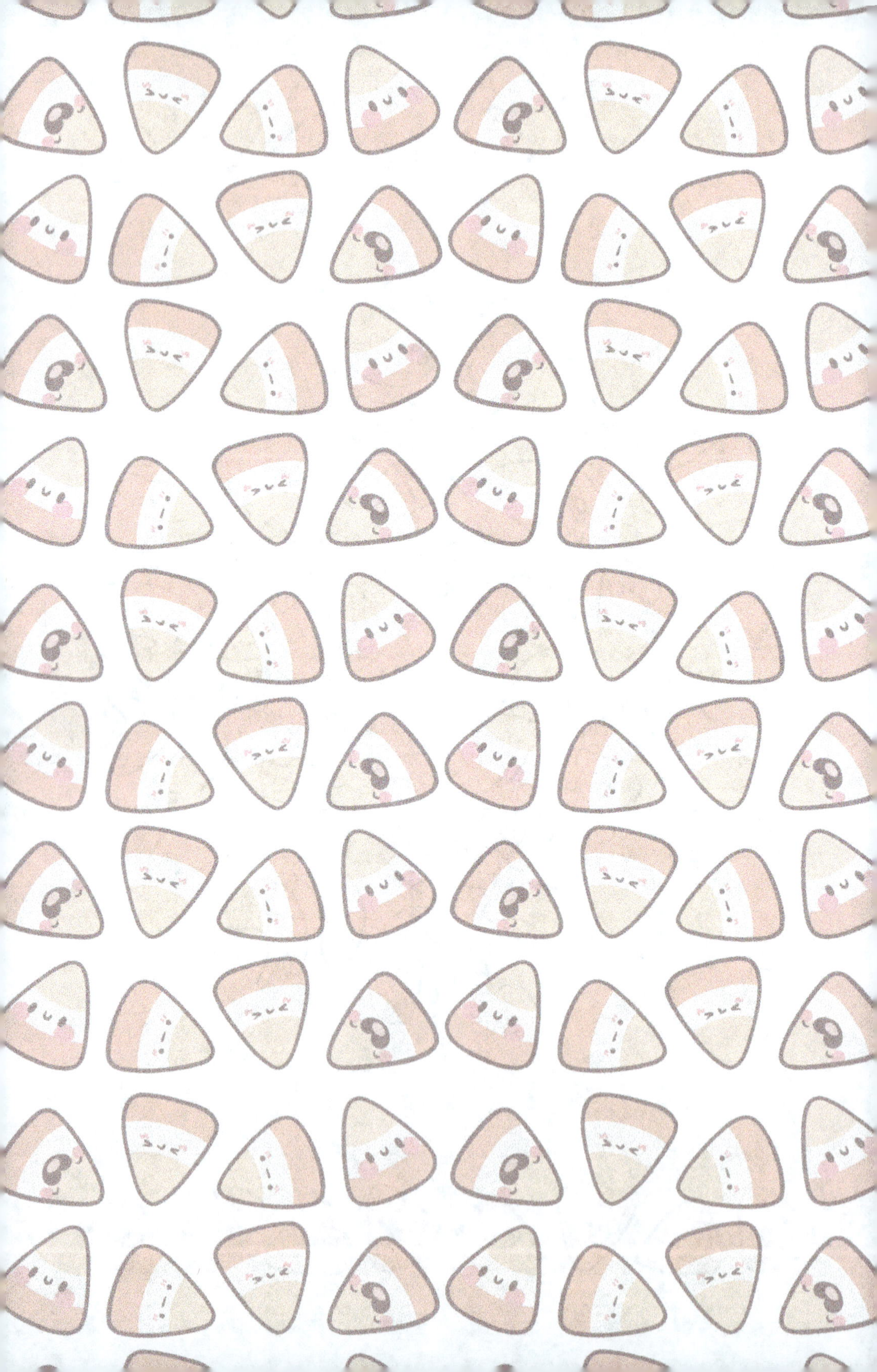

Hello from Pinkee again!

The following are some tutorials that range from beginner to a little more advanced. Each with a cute Halloween theme!

Each tutorial is a step by step process and any that have more than one element each element will have it's own tutorial so you can create each element on it's own and then combine to make your own image.

I do my best to make sure the tutorial include steps that will help with any drawing you make, not just these but future endeavours as well!

For the more advanced tutorials, I do my best to break them down piece by piece. Take your time, and create at your own pace. If you struggle come back to it, no pressure just fun!

Love,
Pinkee

Haunted House Tutorial

Lay down the skeleton of your house. Rectangles, squares and triangles are your best friends for this part!

Add in some of the structural details. I like to put in the windows here but then add some curves to the building itself. It kind of reminds me of a Burton-esque house!

Once you have the main structure
down you can add your little
details to the house. Put shutters
on the windows, maybe they are
not quite straight. Add details
around the door and on the roof
until you get the look you want.

Next, focus on the elements that give it a spooky feeling ... the ghosts floating by, the big full moon or the added roof decorations.

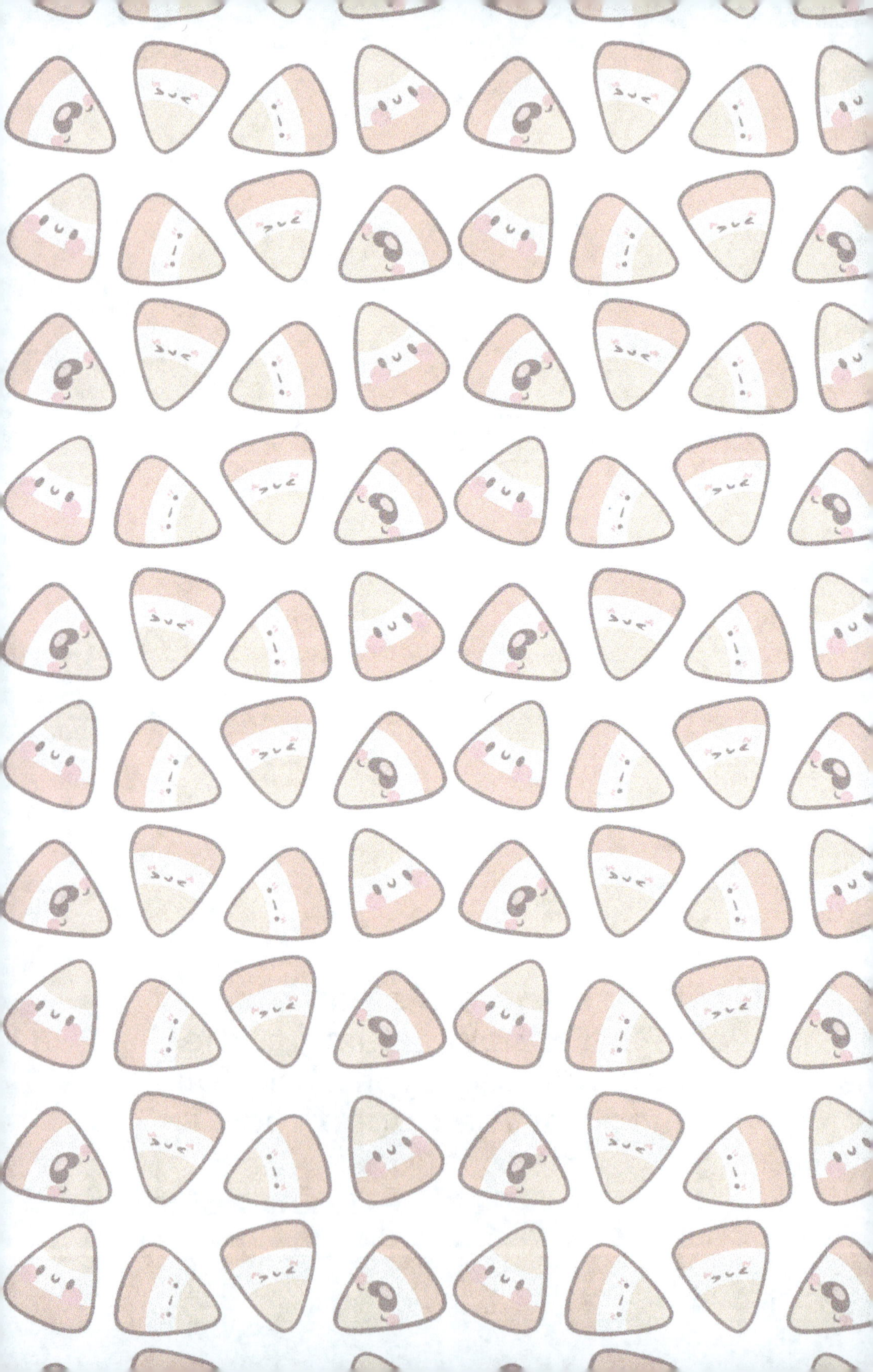

Pumpkin Man Tutorial

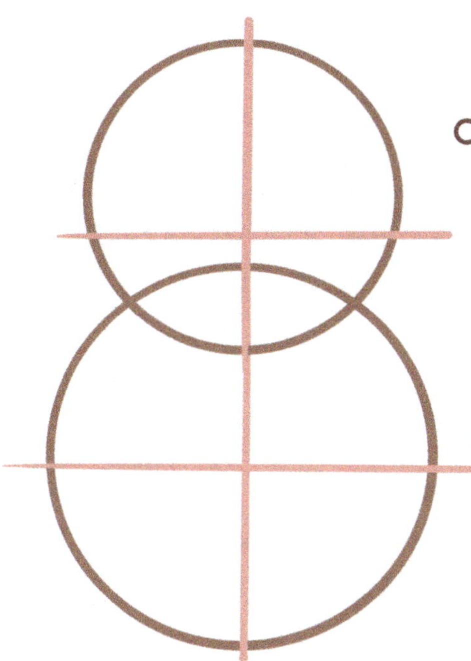

Start with a small circle above a larger circle, then create cross t's for reference.
TIP: Flip it instead and do a larger head on top for an even cuter look!

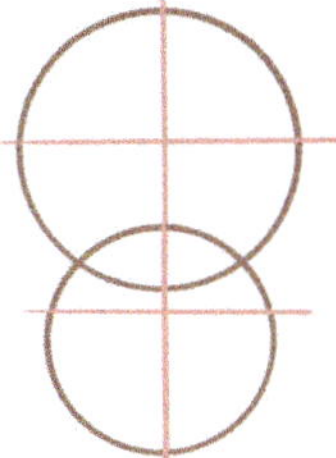

Using the cross t's choose a part that is slightly above the bottom and outside the sides of the circle. Create a slightly schmooshed down bottom of the head and body by using this guide to draw a new bottom to your circles. (That's a technical term.)

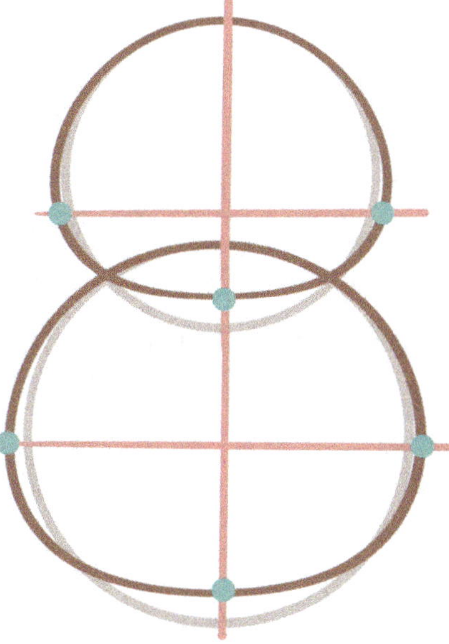

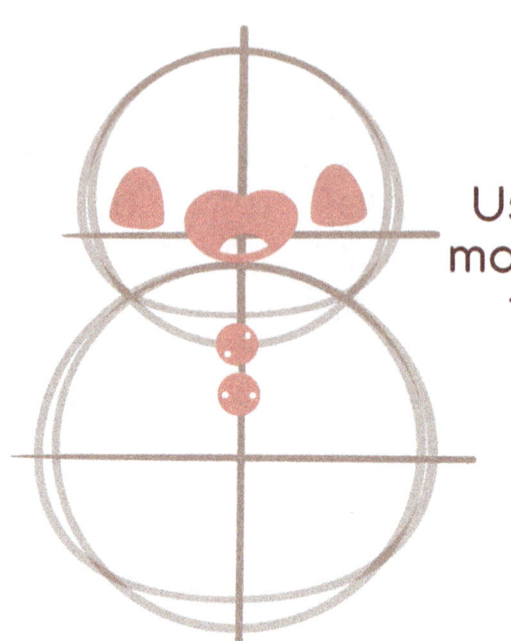

Using those t's we made, add in a cute face and some buttons.

Add a stem and leaves to the top.

Some little curls at the top and don't forget the arms. All done!

TIP: You may need to clean up lines from time to time if your sketch gets a little messy. Feel free to do this at any step of your sketching process!
I don't tend to erase lines completely in case I change my mind later!

Witchy Pumpkin Tutorial

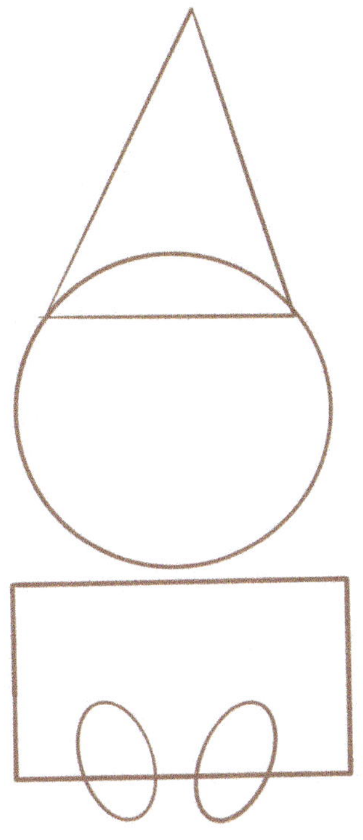

Start with the basic shapes of our little pumpkin witch, a triangle, circle, rectangle and two ovals for the feet.

Next we will build on our skeleton and add a curved rectangle for the scarf, two more triangles for the sleeves and a cross for the face in order to help with our next steps.
TIP: I will sometimes add little details like I did with the feet at this stage so I don't forget about it!

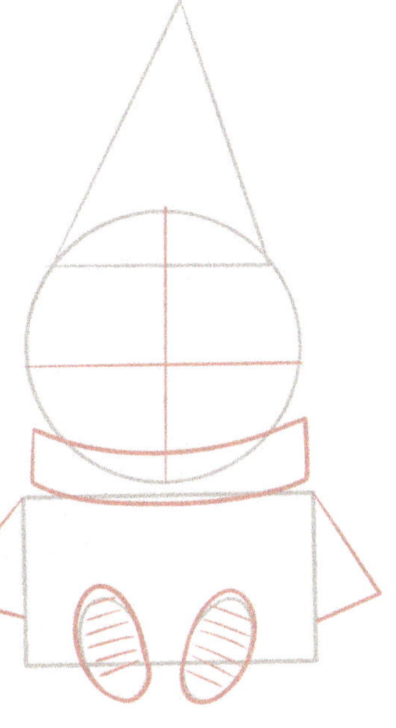

Round out the head using your guides to help. You'll also want to add the bottom of the scarf with tassels if you like. Then fill out the body and scarf by rounding each out a bit.

Next let's focus on the sleeves, again round them out to make them look more like cloth. Then add the shoulders to the scarf and add a face. Finally, let's tackle the hat. Remember to keep things loose. Add a buckle if you like, and a little flop over at the top!

Now onto the meat and potatoes
of the Sweet Halloween
experience!

I love doodle lists, if you follow my
Instagram you will see one for
every month for almost two years
now. So it's no surprise that I will
be adding these as well!

Use the book to sketch in some
doodles for the prompts below.
Each month the whole Pinkee Pal
community joins in and draws
together each day. It's so much
fun and no you don't have to do
each day!
Have fun with these, you never
know what you'll create!

Love,
Pinkee

Pumpkin

Ghost

Witch

Skull

Bat

Spider

Vampire

Zombie

Moon

Owl

Candy

Mask

Potion

Black Cat

Haunted

Broom

Lantern

Tombstone

Creepy

Cauldron

Web

Goblin

Mummy

Fright

Spell

Dark

Monster

Shadow

Phantom

Scream

Candy Corn

Thank You

I hope you have enjoyed this book as much as I have enjoyed doing it with you. Thank you for choosing to spend your time with me.

Tag me @doodleswithpinkee if you share any of your artwork. I'd love to see what you create.

Create
with Pinkee
Sweet Hallowe'en